AQUA

EMBRACE THE SPLASH AS DROPS OF WORDS FORM A POOL OF WISDOM

RAVI VERMA

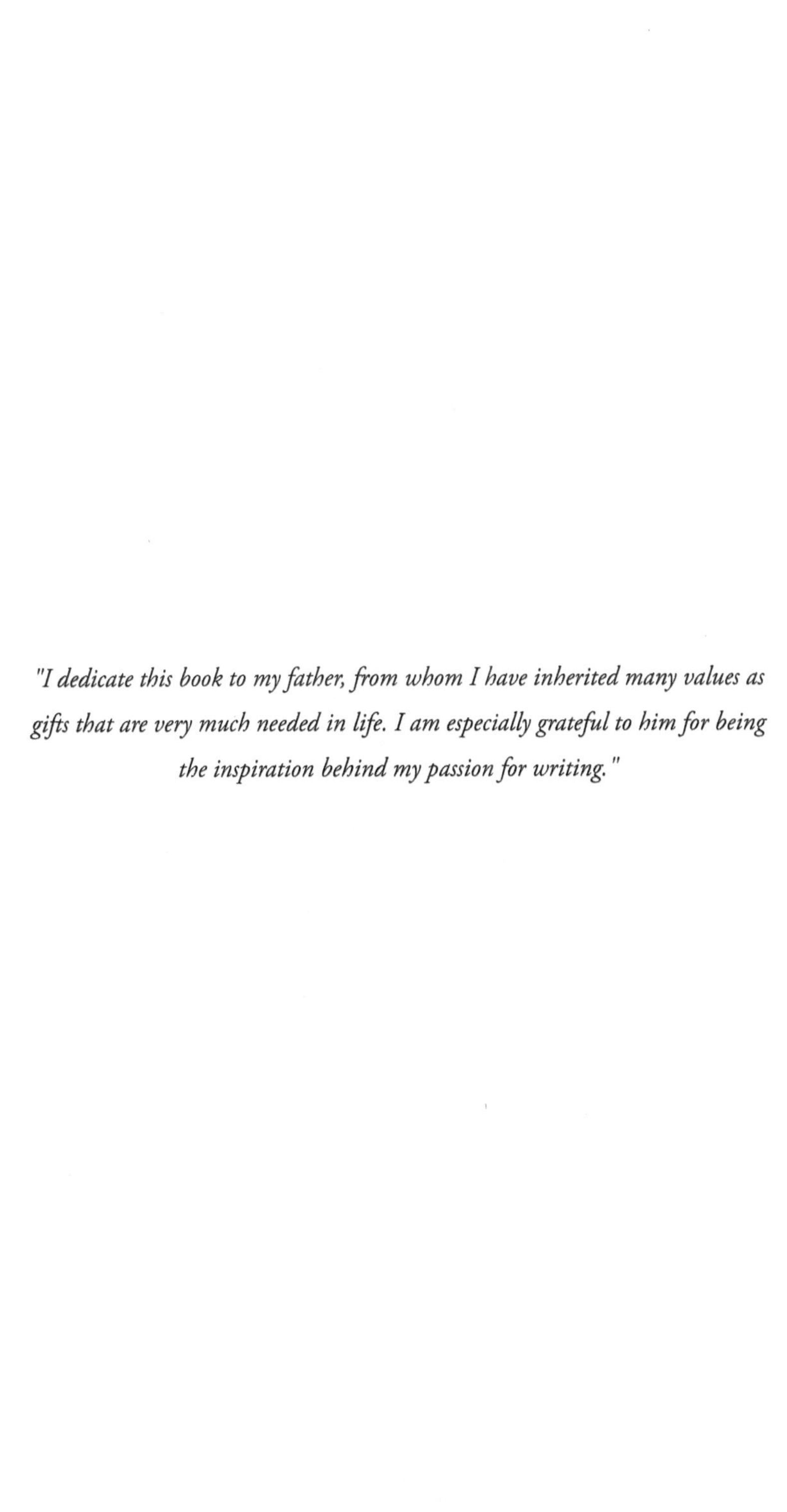

"I dedicate this book to my father, from whom I have inherited many values as gifts that are very much needed in life. I am especially grateful to him for being the inspiration behind my passion for writing."

Contents

Contents

Contents

Contents

Preface

AQUA is the third book published in the series *Embrace*. It inherits the miscellaneous theme from its predecessors and holds the responsibility to take the poetic torch forward.

Embrace helps to maintain a poetic entry of the author's chronological growth, both creatively and personally. With each book you can surely find how the thoughts and ideas have progressed over time as the author gains more experience and sees life happening to him and to others around him.

With pure intentions to share the authors opinions, views, approach, and take on various personal imaginative trips and real worldly issues, situations, cause, and observations, this book is being shared with you Dear Reader.

Author's intentions are always to share positive and optimistic messages through each poem. Even if a poem seems to share negativity or talk about a dark subject, it is written to generate awareness, start a discussion, seek attention on the matter, and give light to the topic. The need is to be aware, forbid, not support, and condemn when such matters come to one's notice.

Take a deep breath and embrace the splash as drops of words form a pool of wisdom.

RAVI VERMA

15-12-2022

Acknowledgements

I would like to acknowledge the following individuals who have contributed in the creation of this book's cover.

Cover Image © Matheo

Instagram : @matheo_jbt

Cover Design by Prakriti Verma

Instagram : @prakver

Beginning Quote

"Never hesitate to initiate as initiation precedes success, and success precedes another initiation."

1. Phoney

What is my worth without the transient lucre?
mundane pride, heart shallow and bitter.
An opaque glow,
an invisible flow.
Lavish walls, though
hideous to know.

2. Condescending

I walk stiff,
head facing above.
Eyes gazing the sky,
planning on purchasing some love.
Mind always coding a lie,
even though heart requests to defy.
A statue dreaming of high stature,
first to blame on the other, never eager to comply.
Pretending to help foreseeing the gain,
never available when needed in pain.
A leech, being a parasite, latching onto its prey,
you are not transparent, but greyer than grey.

3. Pain

I push insecurities out,
plough away unsought sensitivities.
Sprinkle life,
let it rain.
Make way for spring,
thorns stepped upon.
Struggles accompany,
blossoming pain at brim.

4. True Face

I have fallen to a place below,
layers of assumptions and false ego.
Tripping on wires,
scandalous vows.
Presumptions prepping,
for many raised brows.

First Quote

"When hurt, try to acknowledge the cause of pain instead of anxiously trying to get rid of the scar."

5. Having It All

Never have I ever felt,
delight that could fulfil my every object.
The all, I am always searching for,
not sure what that even means at all.
Round or oval, exactly what shape to look for?
whether should I search for it near or far?
The search continues,
and I am still eager for the answers.
Though, I am now unclear of the purpose behind my expedition,
as I move forward, the clock tells me to move on with no explanation.
I am beginning to appreciate more, the gifts I already received,
attentively, I now acknowledge the good I have yielded.
Even if the questions remain unanswered,
I have a feeling I'll end up well-delivered.

6. Surprising Self

I surprised myself!

I landed perfectly fine by myself.

Seems your help was never necessary,

I was enough already.

Not sure why I wasted so much time awaiting your presence,

fate had never proposed to make you the condition for my existence.

Became too comfortable within your make-believe secure boundaries,

forgot how free, sweet, and green independence tastes.

7. Unmotivated Soul

Uninspired,

unmotivated.

pitiful,

hallucinated.

A wanderer wandering with an aimless sight,

betting his luck on nothing but void.

Surfing on hopelessness, waiting,

with no intentions of any effort, laying.

8. Shallow

Are you a friend?
no, I don't think so.
You say you want to help me,
but never standing up for what you see.
Joining others while they bully me,
excusing your actions, saying all this hurt is to bring the best in me.
I am still ignoring,
though it has escalated thereafter.
In attempts of seeking the unpromising popularity,
you are losing someone better.
When in public,
you are nowhere near.
Privately,
you pretend to be the only well-wisher.
Actively mocking when in a herd,
explaining how I seem to be an awfully mindful nerd.
Maybe you are right,
no! you are totally wrong.
I am fine the way I am,
not saying I am perfect.
I do need to improve,
and do need feedbacks.
But you are no guru,
nor a community counsellor.

If you truly meant well,

it would be a private setting.

Not a roast in public,

while pointing at me and acting as if you cannot stop laughing.

Once is fine,

twice I can withstand.

Thrice you need to self-evaluate,

after that no chances.

Goodbye! take care!

I was kind, patient, and empathetic enough already.

Your self-centred ego couldn't analyse?

I feel bad for you, sorry.

You were not ready for the separation?

well, its late now.

I already moved on,

this long you have underestimated, now you need to leave me alone.

Second Quote

"Only the privileged have the ability, the mentality, and the possibility to lose."

9. Assured Relief

A tired brain may want to surrender,
with an exhausted mind it's easier to hinder.
Unseen but keen,
once you believe, faith will lean.
Make sure you retain the hope for better,
relief is assured sooner or later.

10. Pricing Peace

Lost in the hurry,
a lot had to bury.
Though a lot was gained,
although being alive mostly pained.
The pinch of a void never secluded,
haunted by my choices, the guilt never eluded.

11. Not Now

There are many plans for you,

plan A to Z and then again they renew.

No matter what you choose,

what path you let yourself loose.

There will always be another way,

other options than to just runaway.

Have faith in whatever you believe is supreme,

no matter how difficult it may seem.

Your faith will always accompany,

your prayers will keep your attitude in symphony.

The higher energy will do help track your dream,

maybe late but for sure you'll reach your appealing destiny.

Time takes time being always present,

you need to keep hustling until you receive its present.

Remember, time never says no,

it only says not now.

12. Mountain thrower

Challenges seem mere,
not worth any despair.
Heir of the heavenly quintessence,
partisan of the humanely existence.
I was born to achieve great,
great in whatever feels great to my heart and my intellect.
Even failure does not blur the fact that I am special,
to me it proves that the world I am living in is real.

Third Quote

"Negligence roots from one's lack of diligence"

13. Imperfectly Perfect

Unlike God,
I'm an imperfectly perfect bod.
Not the greatest,
but with a unique taste.
I slip few times,
but the slip also slides to success sometimes.
Sometimes I feel not the best,
especially when drowning in front of the rest.
It's easy to stop, so never do so,
pause when needed but make sure that soon you get set, go!
Do not let the first defeat be an excuse for the failure,
it will still be called success even if a recurring venture.
It is okay to fail or to lose,
part of life, cannot elude.

14. Understanding The Assignment

Assignment is clear,
nothing much to bear.
If I ever decide to share,
I want you to just hear.
Be a listener till I conclude,
bringing your pain in between will only cause the session to be
discontinued.
Not always do I need advice,
sometimes I just need solace,
I expect nothing big from thou,
except basic sense and few actions to bestow.

15. Abominable Pain

With reasons unheard,
partially remembered.
Incorrect, facts blurred,
deliberately stirred.
Alone I stood,
in a painful silence, stood misunderstood.

16. Sharing Is Not Always Caring

Your tales have affected perceptions for others,
your own experiences have stopped many other possible connections.
Imaginary characters have been formed as per your stories,
others have started to act realistically upon your misconceived encounter
deliveries.
Once found otherwise, more than trust you could lose,
be mindful and aware, rest is up for you to choose.

Fourth Quote

"To understand and empathize is human, to not ignore in ignorance is divine."

17. Seeking Actions After Apologies

Just acknowledging a wound,
never tames the pain.
To heal it sound,
some actions need to be taken.
Sorry can be said three times in a second,
meaningless it becomes, the moment it is the second.
You can slap again and then say sorry,
wouldn't make a difference to this cruel story.

18. Within

Weave within the trust,
agreement of an incessant self-love.
In silence,
find your own voice.
Dwell in your dreams of dreamy dreams,
give time to self, a hopeful presence.

19. Easy Breezy

Touch-me-not?
just try to touch me again.
I may seem easy,
I chose to be that way.
But to think I'll always be that breezy,
it's a price you'll have to pay.

20. Road Taken

Why doesn't the guilt fade away?
even as time passes by, it stays there somewhere the same old way.
Holding my steps whenever they weaken,
reminding me of the bruises caused due to the same old reason.
The story could have been different,
possible endings to the tale were in fact abundant.
Though, I take pride in who I became,
as I belong to the roads I myself had taken.

Fifth Quote

"Better stabilize expectations as expectations can weaken stability."

21. Singular Power

With no one beside,
just a strong mind ready to stride.
It still feels okay,
with a determined psyche, it doesn't seem that grey.
A voice deep inside caresses,
an empowering courage traverses.

22. It's In You

A piece in me somewhere
was eager to find the peace I lost nowhere.
Far I searched,
couldn't find any trace.
It was in me,
waiting for me to embrace.

23. I The Centre

I, the beauty,

I, the truth.

Rest just seem pretty,

pretty till, still a handful of wealth.

I, the centre,

I, the strength.

Mortal entity might prefer luxury,

luxury wouldn't soothe all the emptiness or the hunger.

24. Toxic Masculinity

You hate pink?
this I bet is a big lie.
A feminine choice?
you're such an insecure guy.
A mirror to your obsession,
these stances are a reflection.
Observe the toxicity before it spreads,
paralyzing your intellect, venomous thought process.

Sixth Quote

"Stop trying to shape yourself in a way others want you to be like. Putting unsuitable pressure can crack, disfigure, or even break a piece or a person at some point."

25. Not Worth

Unlike your observations,
I am not among the ones to be swiftly persuaded.
Feel sorry for your vindictive losses,
I stand steady on the ground, little to no chances to be swayed.
It ain't worth to waste your unvaluable time trying to shape my thoughts,
you should probably find something else in which you might be better of
course.
Not playing with your ego, I'm trying to show you the reality,
unfamiliar to you, some people do care about others in perfect sense of
actuality.

26. Personal Recommendations

Please ignore, Ignored,
but still followed.
Do repent, Repented,
but still reminded.
Advices adhered,
not always aided.
Blaming self for the bad,
always misled.
The one who or which followed,
needed an action against and not ignorance.
The one who or which reminded,
needed to let go before any lost memorable reverence.
Aid comes from within,
as acceptance dims sorrow,
Feeling of healing you take in,
there will be a better tomorrow.

27. Hope And Only Hope

Sufficed once,
now obsolete.
Graph of relevance,
a capricious feat.
Pride and tide,
always retreats.
When everything looks hazed,
only hope relieves.

28. Shattered Innocence

When light withdraws,
evil surrounds.
Help gathers,
denial answers.
Immature maturity,
claims superiority.
Maneuvers mumble,
wisdom rumbled.
An agreement to gamble,
ruins resembled.

Seventh Quote

"We ignore, console, and hide when it's about us but focus, dissuade, and persuade when it's about the others."

29. Empty The Bins

Empty these bins of your mind,
stench from these is giving feeling of an insecure find.
Attempts of keeping them hidden,
resulted in this dumpyard being rotten, but not forgotten.
You do know,
you need to let these go.
One day surely,
you need to free yourself from all this self-doubt and unnecessary humility.
Knowing what others think of you,
doesn't help much in securing your individuality.
Consider yourself an asset,
crucial part of this world, only you are good at things you know, love to
do, and are best at.
Shut the outside noise,
not your inner voice.

30. Sure Enough

Patiently wait while hustling the weight,
chores in this world were never straight.
Your efforts matter and won't ever go uncounted,
Somewhere ahead you'll definitely get them rounded.
Even if you lose, regain the heed,
sure enough, you'll succeed indeed.

31. Chandeliers

A loser in daylight,
but luxurious by night.
Desires never suffice,
but lifetime recedes with time.
Shiny polished surface,
stashing pain of a lifetime.
No matter the appreciations during the day I collect,
an image of closeted emotions at night recollect.

32. Shadowed Trouble

Troubled by doubts I uncovered myself,
an unsettled unrest devoured my patience.
I acted foolishly, proved self's wrong, felt guilty for unvalued stuff,
was eager to find and believe in something awfully nonsense.
Lack of trust on my own,
brought the tears and fears of unexpected unknown.
To deal with this shadowed trouble,
I had to first acknowledge me for being terrible.
My ignorance and inconfidence messed my state,
prioritising and loving self then made a positive impact.

Eighth Quote

"Peace comes to those who follow and favor the right,

least ease comes to those who ridicule but savor the fight."

33. Fern

Coiled up,
waiting to flower.
Curiosity rises up,
desires fly higher.
Pinnate figure,
I resemble a kind.
Pips not needed,
I was a spore that travelled here by air.
Different, I know,
I look artistic while I grow.
Still, we all have a similar purpose,
to support existence of one another.
Nurture life's core nature,
continue to respect the fundamentals of nature.

34. Consoling Past

When memories of the past pay me a visit,
somehow all the merry moments get filtered out.
What's left to contemplate upon?
whys, what's, and how's then dawn.
Guilt tortures the desire to feel good,
continuous mental assault affects my mood.
Tired of this battle where in any case I failed,
No matter what I thought, only grief impressioned.
If this continues, my present would suffer,
I decided then to let go and stop consoling my past forever.

35. The Aftermath

When the storm rages,
distress floods.
Chaotic disarray disperses,
helplessness and confusion surges.
Wants mean nothing,
needs seem everything.
To save or to be saved,
expectations and goals become uncomplicated.
When the storm perishes,
hope sprouts.
Grief and relief emerges,
healing and renewing commences.
Comfort transcends to being luxurious,
affluence recites its rights for privileges.
Oaths govern the decisions,
memorials for tax implications.

36. A Shelter Is All I Need

Wandering,

with an awry frail physique,

I am still searching.

Searching for a place with nothing more but some shadow,

if lucky, a little water to wet my choking throat,

an edible taste to my painful hunger.

Hunger has been haunting my entire existence,

from trash or some heir's ashet,

scavenging dream of a fully fed belly.

Belly has been sinking under,

even the kind-hearted ones now maintain distance and disappear.

Disappear within closed doors,

do not answer my bells but wipe the switch I touched later,

leaving me with hope more weaker and eager.

Eager to be helped,

but the untouchable me seeks for no sympathy.

Sympathy is of no use for me,

advices to work for a living have been flooding my ears from the

beginning.

Beginning till end,

I am not ranting for you to feel sorry,

I am just telling you for being remembered as me vanishing won't be a

recorded story.

Ninth Quote

"Once I am able to assure and satisfy the voices within, rest all then just becomes noise."

37. Traumatic Happiness

I have always been wished and preached to be happy,
being happy always was taught to be the ultimate way to live.
No other way than to be invariably merry,
being contended unfailingly, the only reason worth being alive.
Compared with others who had their happiness showcased,
crying underneath, but with a big animated laughter they faked.
In moments not good, made to feel as having a life unsatisfactory,
a low phase temporary, described to be a continuous state of misery.
All of which I found were untrue,
a reality check with myself is all I had to do.
How distinct could a torch light up in daylight?
with no darkness there would be no reverence for the sunlight.

38. Valley

A stream of freshness,
oozing from the springs of divine greatness.
Trickle down the gigantic rocks,
caressing land, fostering the folks.
Calming sound of the dancing water,
irrigates hope, portraying life lively and greener.

39. Truth Falsely Implied

What you hear isn't always what was said,
meaning might differ on whether you're happy, mad or sad.
Understanding stands balanced upon the state of mind,
an unhappy spirit expects only a desolate find.
An ongoing battle with self it is,
triggering solicitation of self-loathing validations.
Voices within are louder than expected,
as per the mood, a version of the theory gets elected.
One has to validate purpose and only then take measures,
pay attention to priorities and then plan retaliations.

40. Kindness Ripples

Kindness ripples heart to heart,
actions of consideration always leave their mark.
To be kind doesn't take much,
nothing sacrificial or demanding as such.
A selfless action, an interaction with someone down to earth,
even an effortless smile can ignite warmth.
From one to the other,
effects of goodwill shared further.

Tenth Quote

"Like a tree, feel free to spread roots wherever and whenever a possibility."

41. Planting Hope

A curious soul in the vicinity of moisture,
knits dreams of a wondrous future.
Even though in darkness,
motivation from hope its spirit harnesses.
Patiently waits as time passes by,
outgrows darkness, only on imagination no more to rely.
Darkness now succeeded by a cosmic palette,
with newest wings, the dreams soar furthest.

42. Dear Bear

Dear bear,
you okay?
I know it's hard to bear,
but what else can I say than to just pray.
Oh, so your house was looted as well?
besides the execution, they beheaded your pal?
What more to say,
You shouldn't have taken the wrong way.
Humans by birth are that way,
you should've been careful anyway.
You no more inhabit the old address, moved to the city?
good for you to choose the new enclosed facility.

43. Handle With Care

Delicate beings have delicate feelings,
thoughtful expressions in action share deeper meanings.
Wise interactions soothe troubled thoughts,
considerate behavior loosens sheepish knots.
Kind gestures sprout compassionate motives,
only solicited remarks become reverable advices.

44. I Am The Ocean

I am the ocean,
my depth is unexplored.
I am the ocean,
my magnificence can't be ignored.
Have hidden treasures,
resourceful pleasures.
Thoughts living their life herein,
emerging, growing, forming, also transforming out and within.
Tides of great heights dwindling,
again with force further beyond rising.

Eleventh Quote

"Why do I need to change always if you are the one getting bothered?"

45. Reality Check

Expecting selflessness is selfishness as well,
when asked about their entitlement, entitled minds own no rationale.
'It's just how it is', they say,
funny how owning two cars out of the millions makes them to think this
way.
When your circle is small, likewise, and limited,
your range of thinking and knowing gets restricted.
Experience beyond to think beyond,
with a rainbow of colors, more colors can be formed.

46. Similar Us

Not the same but similar indeed,
preferences different but with the same fundamental needs.
Striving alone but working together,
attempts to succeed easier with the support of one another.

Human beings humanely motivated,
understanding that harmony is long belated.
In accordance to the existential essence,
nature's delicate symbiotic existence.

47. Emotional Forgery

Why'd you lie to me?
when you could've chosen the route of honesty.
Why break my trust on you?
when you could've loosen only a little till the bond could've felt fine to
renew.
How magnificent,
this behavior reticent.
This seems like a game for you,
you seem to be a skilled player.
This skill sadly,
can only help in carrying out emotional forgery.
No long-term benefit it promises in reality,
only ephemeral moments of false splendour possibly.

48. Explore The Wilderness

A naive wonderer began wondering alone,
with previous experience of lone survival, none.
Expecting to experience nothing wrong,
assuming the troubles won't come along.
Aspirations of following and promoting only the good ways,
trusting and treating everyone nicely always.
Gullible being, easily targeted,
once fooled, over and over again persuaded.
Learnt lessons the hard way,
recessiveness is preyed upon in every way.
The world only cares for possible prospects,
rest get ignored until they fight for their rights or protest.

Twelfth Quote

"Learn to say **no**. Prioritizing yourself isn't selfish, it's ratheran affirmation of self-worth."

49. Safe And Sound

When you first started to care if I was safe and sound,
then the strong bond between us I thought was actually found.
Since then, all I ever cared about is to be aware of your whereabouts.
ideas that tried to tell an alternate story I fought.
All I ever hoped for, kept patience and the will to wait more,
is a testament of the love I believed I should ensure.
Bedtime prayers requesting light for you,
specific dreams every night fighting against the notions I thought were
untrue.
While being selfless and blind,
I never cared to care for my self and my mind.
Not thinking that if you leave me one day,
I'll be left alone in despair, with just myself I'll have to stay.

50. Vermarine Or Aquamarine

This or that,
just on luck you shouldn't bet.
You shouldn't assume to have only a single choice,
with enough efforts you can have options more than twice.
There's no limit unless you yourself think so,
if you can't even fathom the possibilities, there won't be any hope for more
also.
Take your capabilities into consideration,
your abilities aren't bounded, relieve yourself of every restrictive or
excusive reason.

51. Sun

I want to be a positive ray of light,
emanate aura bright like daylight.
Foster sunshine,
spread joy no matter whether it's the night-time, morning or noon.
Mould myself in a way that when the light outside would brightly shine,
so would my inner sheen.
A caregiver to the dimmed inclinations,
saving from the unpleasant inflictions.

52. Dandelions

Thirteenth Quote

"We all are innately strong,

each breath we take has been testifying this notion for so long."

53. Celebrate Life

In quest for more and better,
we keep on losing peace.
While competing for attaining nicer,
we forget that time's not losing pace.
Every now and then take a pause,
make sure to remind yourself of the actual cause.
Reason to start this hustle was to survive,
but it became more about the desire to portray and less about the desire to
live.
Bring your consciousness back to reality,
before it's too late to even acknowledge the truth partly.
Whatever and whoever has appeared will disappear one day,
no exception to the certainty even if you'd pray.

54. Turquoise Dream

When together,
wonders flower.
Strength appears,
courage volunteers.
Fewer fears,
comforted tears.
Diffidence evades,
cynicism fades.

Green and blue,
or yellow and blue.
when mixed together,
creates a dreamy color.
Turquoise dream,
an enigma supreme.
Visual pleasure,
serene leisure.

55. Wake Up

Change isn't comfortable,
the uneasy feeling it embodies is relatable.
Stagnant mind reeks of stubbornness,
dwindling likeability and shrewdness.
Acceptance of our oblivious behavior,
marks the initial step of acknowledging and embracing the true humane-
nature.
Extend your thinking and facilitate progressive thoughts,
welcome change and possible reforms.

56. Not Asking Much

Speak not,

just listen.

Worry not,

just pay attention.

Words do not soothe enough as much as the silence sometimes,

emotionally flooded sense can get overwhelmed with even a well-intended

advice.

Aching heart seeks consoling eyes,

sometimes harmless solicitous lies.

Not asking much,

just a compassionate behavior and no judgements as such.

Fourteenth Quote

"Grief is a mental, emotional, physical, and psychological tsunami triggered by the displacement of a large volume of support, care, affection, and the company of someone or something, leaving everlasting effects."

57. Searing Caring Words

Made-up masks of friendly advices,
may sometimes hide the truth and the real vices.
What may seem to be a thoughtful gesture,
could really be a tactic to achieve a personal desire.
Seeming kind actions,
often enslave possible suspicions.
We forget that the words said own a strange property,
they can mean different with different state and comprehensible ability.

58. Closer To The Finish Line

Hold on to the dream,
remember, hope is supreme.
Few more steps left to cover,
not the time for morale to lower.
Remind yourself the true purpose,
let the idea of success be your motivational stimulus.
Quitting now will be a big disappointment,
know that your progress till now is a validation that you're resilient.

59. Back To The Basics

A sensible notion reflects sense,
projecting one's intelligence.
Neglected reality doesn't fade away,
it stays put until you finally undertake.
Meaning might change but not the effects of it,
what's said, already did, hurt doesn't acquit.
Honesty accompanies solace,
sense of unconcerned bliss, joy of independence.

60. Aqua

Two drops of different hue,

both in search of a distinctive name other than blue,

stepped on a new journey to explore,

about to break stereotypes, never attempted before.

Unlike the rest in their community,

they agreed upon the idea of one's own individuality.

Once they escaped their social quod,

together they formed a tiny squad.

Surviving alone without a secure fort,

they each realised their unique forte.

Though they had won few battles alone,

but when together, failure was always prone.

Lesson of unity was learnt this way,

one chose to change and the other remained the same way.

Green and blue were they then called,

accepted choices of each other, their success hauled.

An old legend says, 'together we shine',

even to preserve a pickle, you need at least two ingredients for a brine.

When green and blue combine,

then forms aquamarine.

Fifteenth Quote

"The one who invests should be the one who harvests. But in life sadly, *should* is more frequent than *would*."

About The Author

Ravi Verma

He is an Indian Writer and a Software Engineer. Born on 15 December 2000. Brought up in Indian-Tibetan society as his father Dr. Kanta Prasad Verma was posted as a Teacher at Central School for Tibetans which is an educational institution working as a step to help Tibetan refugees by educating them and helping to conserve their identity, culture, and tradition. Being a job that required the family to move to different parts of India, Ravi has gained a fair share of travel experiences since childhood. He mostly lived in the Hill stations which explains his love and reverence for nature. Previously, his work mostly talked about nature and the effects of human interference. His latest creations on the other hand showcase poetic work mostly focusing on the topics such as hope, faith, self-love, acceptance, and personal and interpersonal human behavior. Lately, his favorite topic to discuss is anything that may relate to the individuality quotient.

You can follow him on:

Instagram: **@ravivermawriter**

Twitter: **@ravivermawriter**

Facebook: **@writerraviverma**

About The Book

Books in the series *Embrace* were originally planned to be published with no more than a year of gap. But due to some certain and even some uncertain events, the author could not publish **AQUA** in the year 2021.

Instead of publishing a book in the series Embrace, the Year 2021 was dedicated to introducing other poetry book series, namely *Unconditional* and *Purposes*. MiniBook **Amour-Propre** was published as the first-ever book in the series *Unconditional.* Mini Book **Finding Me** from the series *Purposes* on the other hand is available for pre-order and is planned to be made available soon.

Now, after almost two years of the gap from the last published book **SPROUTS** in the series Embrace, the author is anxiously excited and ready to share his latest creations in this book.

Take your time and enjoy!

A Note Expressing Gratitude

"Thank you for investing your time and reading this book. I hope you were able to embrace the refreshing and replenishing splash as drops of words formed a pool of wisdom. Wish you all the very best in all your present and future endeavors. Thank you once again!

Would love to hear/read your thoughts on the book and connect with you."

You can connect with me on:
Instagram: **@ravivermawriter**
Twitter: **@ravivermawriter**
Facebook: **@writerraviverma**

Ending Quote

"Each commencement plays its part in establishing more confidence as well as experience for future onsets."